D1305655

FY2014 Library Services and Technology Act (LSTA)
Grant titled:

Another Opportunity for
Back to Books

Awarded by the Illinois State Library (ISL), a Division of the
Office of Secretary of State, using funds provided by the Institute
of Museum and Library Services (IMLS).

INVESTIGATING THE
GLOBAL
CLIMATE

INTRODUCTION TO EARTH SCIENCE

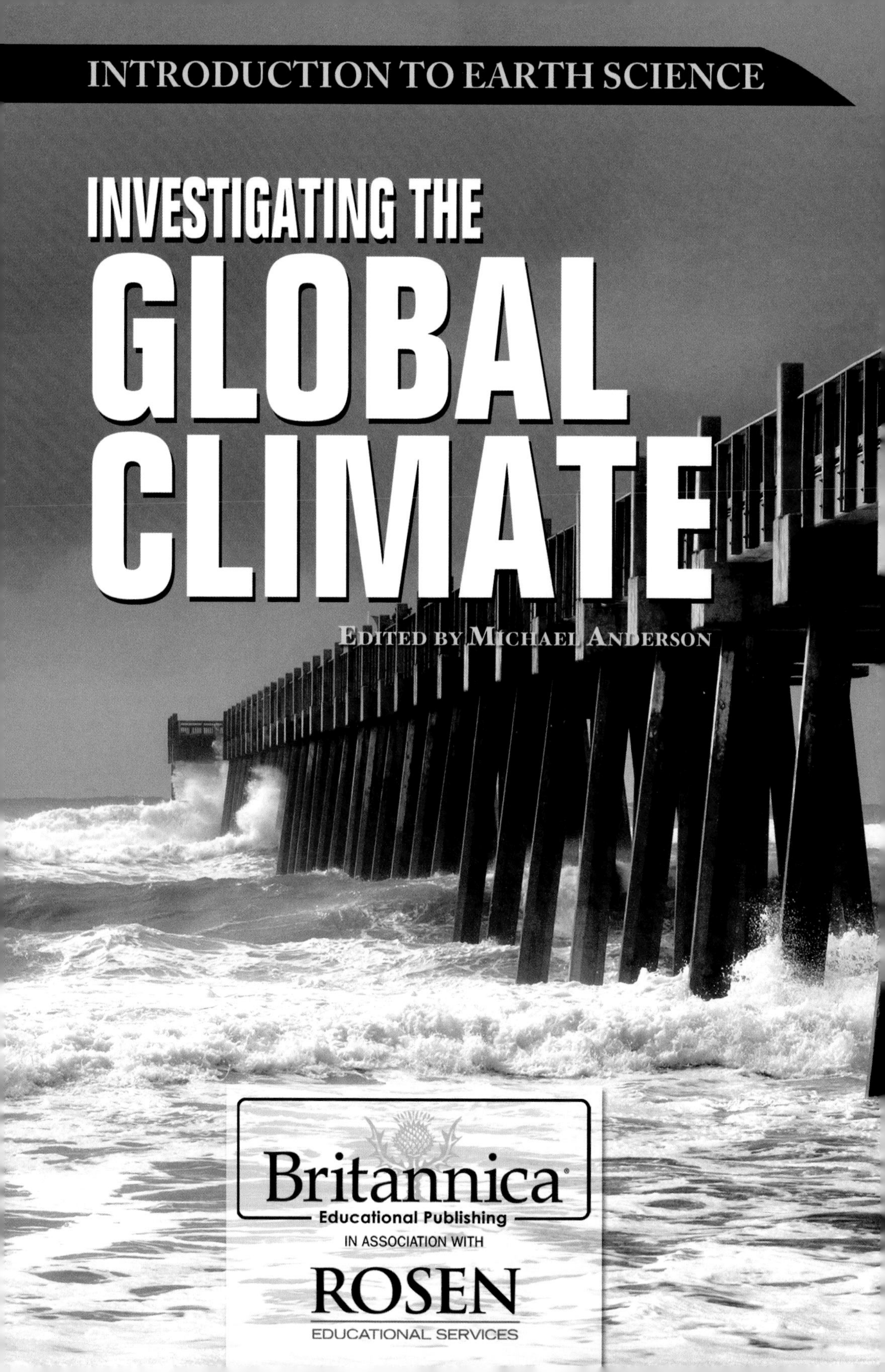

INVESTIGATING THE GLOBAL CLIMATE

EDITED BY MICHAEL ANDERSON

Britannica Educational Publishing
IN ASSOCIATION WITH
ROSEN
EDUCATIONAL SERVICES

Published in 2012 by Britannica Educational Publishing
(a trademark of Encyclopædia Britannica, Inc.)
in association with Rosen Educational Services, LLC
29 East 21st Street, New York, NY 10010.

First Edition

Britannica Educational Publishing
Michael I. Levy: Executive Editor, Encyclopædia Britannica
J.E. Luebering: Director, Core Reference Group, Encyclopædia Britannica
Adam Augustyn: Assistant Manager, Encyclopædia Britannica

Anthony L. Green: Editor, Compton's by Britannica
Michael Anderson: Senior Editor, Compton's by Britannica
Sherman Hollar: Associate Editor, Compton's by Britannica

Marilyn L. Barton: Senior Coordinator, Production Control
Steven Bosco: Director, Editorial Technologies
Lisa S. Braucher: Senior Producer and Data Editor
Yvette Charboneau: Senior Copy Editor
Kathy Nakamura: Manager, Media Acquisition

Rosen Educational Services
Shalini Saxena: Editor
Nelson Sá: Art Director
Cindy Reiman: Photography Manager
Matthew Cauli: Designer
Introduction by Shalini Saxena

Library of Congress Cataloging-in-Publication Data

Investigating the global climate / edited by Michael Anderson.—1st ed.
    p. cm.—(Introduction to earth science)
"In association with Britannica Educational Publishing, Rosen Educational Services."
Includes bibliographical references and index.
ISBN 978-1-61530-496-7 (lib. bdg.)
1. Global temperature changes—Juvenile literature. 2. Climatic changes—Juvenile literature.
I. Anderson, Michael, 1972–
QC903.I586 2012
551.6—dc22

                                                                                    2010048535

Manufactured in the United States of America

On the cover, page 3: Waves caused by a hurricane in the Gulf of Mexico crash into a pier at Pensacola
Beach in Florida. Hurricanes are a type of cyclonic storm common to the humid subtropical climate
of the southeastern United States and to other regions of the world. *John Coletti/The Image Bank/
Getty Images*

Interior background © www.istockphoto.com/Hougaard Malan

551.6
INV

2267514

CONTENTS

When we picture a location, its most distinguishing geographic and cultural landmarks—the Grand Canyon or the Eiffel Tower, for instance—are frequently the first things to come to mind. What may seem less apparent is the climate, although it is also indispensable to our understanding of a particular area. Climate has played a large part in crafting the land and shaping the way life evolved in a place, and it continues to shape our interactions with the landscape. Visiting the pyramids of Giza, to take just one example, would be a vastly different experience without Egypt's arid desert climate as a backdrop. This volume provides a thorough introduction to the climate regions of the world and examines what accounts for those global variations.

A region's climate is influenced by a number of factors and cannot simply be determined by glancing at the weather forecast on any given day. Rather, climate describes the aggregate weather of a place over a period of years and is governed by controls such as latitude, land and water distribution, atmospheric pressure, altitude, and ocean currents, to name a few. The most common measures of climate include mean (average) values of temperature and precipitation such as rain and snow. Comparing various locations using measures like these reveals the

This true color satellite image depicts land covered in vegetation in green, arid areas in brown, snow-covered areas in white, and water in blue. The largely green central landmass, representing the North American continent, contrasts with the white landmasses, representing Greenland and northern Canada, demonstrating the varying climates affecting different regions of the world. Planet Observer/Universal Images Group/Collection Mix: Subjects/Getty Images

incredible range of weather conditions that affect the planet.

This diversity is reflected in the various systems for classifying climates. While regions can be identified in many different ways, dividing the world into climatic zones based on similarities in temperature, precipitation, and vegetation helps reveal patterns between otherwise disparate areas. The classification scheme used in this book takes all of these factors into account and illustrates how, for example, southern California, southern Europe, and the southern coasts of Africa and Australia—separated by thousands of miles of land and ocean—can all share a Mediterranean climate.

The impact of climate on the natural world and human life is wide-ranging and varies from region to region. Generally, however, climate most directly affects vegetation and soils. This in turn can influence settlement patterns and other human activities such as agriculture, which is fundamental to our survival. Technological responses to climate such as central heating, air conditioning, and irrigation have been developed as adaptations to extreme temperatures or aridity.

Such adaptations are inadequate, however, to deal with the climatic phenomenon known as global warming. Although climate describes long-term weather conditions, it should not be viewed as static or constant. While Earth's overall climate has remained stable enough over the course of its history to support life, it has gone through periods of great change—for example, alternating between ice ages and periods of warmth. Global warming is the name given to the rapid rise of air temperatures near Earth's surface over the past century, which scientists have attributed to human causes. Global warming threatens many of the planet's ecosystems and must be managed at an international level through innovative strategies and policies.

While weather is frequently a topic of conversation, it is only part of a larger discussion. Understanding climate and the long-term effects of weather conditions provides a unique perspective on the development of both the geographical and cultural landscapes of the world. And as long as global warming continues to endanger the environment, understanding climate and its effect on the planet will continue to be of vital importance.

The aggregate, long-term weather—or state of the atmosphere—of any place is known as its climate. For example, a description of weather might be "It rained yesterday in Phoenix," while "Phoenix gets only 10 inches of rain per year" would be a statement about climate. Descriptions of climate include such weather elements as temperature, precipitation, humidity, wind, cloudiness, and snow cover. The study of climate is known as climatology. A variety of statistical measures and classification systems have been introduced over the years to help illuminate how climate impacts different regions across the world.

CLIMATE STATISTICS

A location's climate can be described by various statistical measures of the elements of weather and climate. Mean, or average, values are usually computed for a fairly long time period, such as 30 years. These means are often calculated for each month and for the year as a whole.

Extreme maximum and minimum figures help convey the degree of climate variability. Information on the frequency of various events, such as the number of days per year with thunderstorms or the number of frosts in a typical winter, is also important.

Temperature is one of the most important climate elements. Daily mean temperatures may be computed as the average of the daily maximum and minimum temperatures or as the average of temperatures from all 24 hours. These daily means can then be used to compute the mean value for a given month

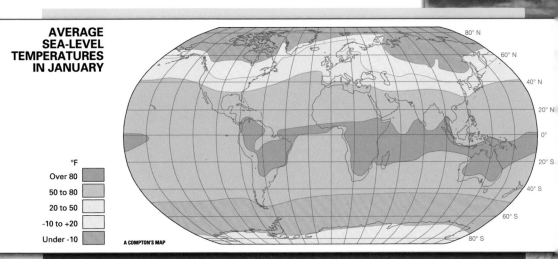

AVERAGE
SEA-LEVEL
TEMPERATURES
IN JANUARY

°F
Over 80
50 to 80
20 to 50
-10 to +20
Under -10

A COMPTON'S MAP

80° N
60° N
40° N
20° N
0°
20° S
40° S
60° S
80° S

A map of mean global surface temperatures for January shows the values adjusted to indicate what the temperatures would be if all the locations were at sea level. (To convert from degrees Fahrenheit to degrees Celsius, subtract 32 and then divide by 1.8.)

or for the entire year. Normal daily maximum and minimum temperatures for a given date or month are also frequently cited. The average difference between nighttime low temperatures and afternoon highs may be less than 10 °F (6 °C) in cloudy climates or at sea but over 30 °F (17 °C) in deserts. The highest and lowest temperatures ever recorded at a site give an idea of the range of temperatures one might experience living a lifetime in that location.

Precipitation data are also very important in describing a location's climate. Mean

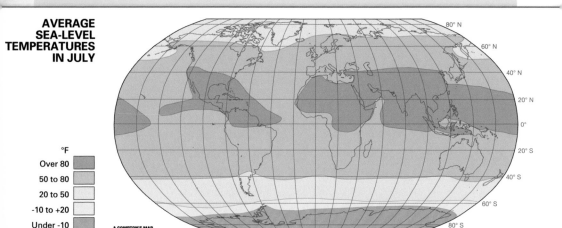

**AVERAGE
SEA-LEVEL
TEMPERATURES
IN JULY**

°F

Over 80
50 to 80
20 to 50
-10 to +20
Under -10

A COMPTON'S MAP

80° N
60° N
40° N
20° N
0°
20° S
40° S
60° S
80° S

A map of mean global surface temperatures for July shows the values adjusted to indicate what the temperatures would be if all the locations were at sea level. (To convert from degrees Fahrenheit to degrees Celsius, subtract 32 and then divide by 1.8.)

and extreme monthly amounts are often cited, with snow often included as "liquid equivalent" precipitation. Snow cover and evaporation data are also important. Mean wind speed and prevailing direction, humidity, and daily hours of sunshine help complete the climate picture.

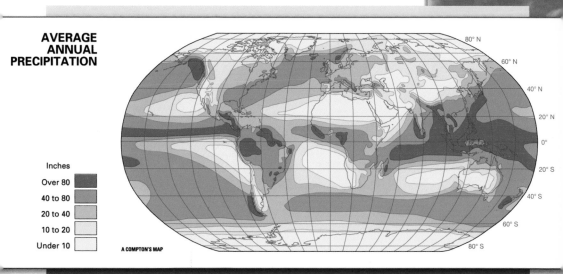

AVERAGE ANNUAL PRECIPITATION

Inches
- Over 80
- 40 to 80
- 20 to 40
- 10 to 20
- Under 10

A COMPTON'S MAP

80° N
60° N
40° N
20° N
0°
20° S
40° S
60° S
80° S

A map shows the mean global distribution of annual precipitation. (One inch equals 2.54 cm.)

CLASSIFICATION OF CLIMATES

No two locations have precisely the same climate, but there are many useful schemes for classifying climates. The ancient Greeks devised a simple scheme. Noting the relationship

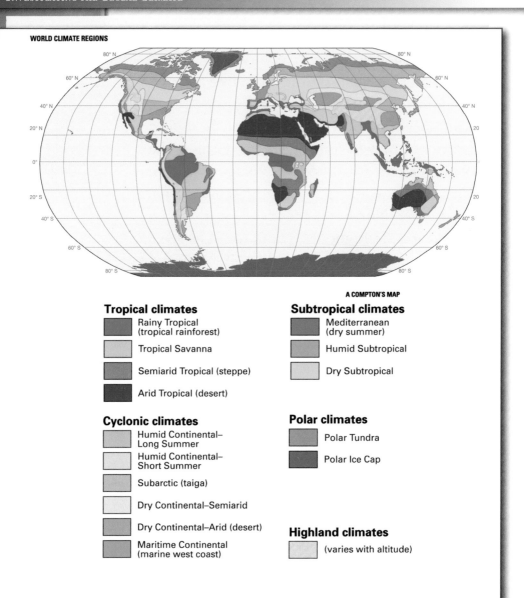

WORLD CLIMATE REGIONS

A COMPTON'S MAP

Tropical climates
- Rainy Tropical (tropical rainforest)
- Tropical Savanna
- Semiarid Tropical (steppe)
- Arid Tropical (desert)

Cyclonic climates
- Humid Continental–Long Summer
- Humid Continental–Short Summer
- Subarctic (taiga)
- Dry Continental–Semiarid
- Dry Continental–Arid (desert)
- Maritime Continental (marine west coast)

Subtropical climates
- Mediterranean (dry summer)
- Humid Subtropical
- Dry Subtropical

Polar climates
- Polar Tundra
- Polar Ice Cap

Highland climates
- (varies with altitude)

The climate regions of the world are based on patterns of average precipitation, average temperature, and natural vegetation. They include tropical, subtropical, cyclonic, polar, and highland climates.

between temperature and latitude, they divided Earth into five broad east-west zones, or *klima*: two frigid polar zones, two temperate midlatitude zones, and a torrid tropical zone. One frigid zone lay in the Northern Hemisphere within the Arctic Circle, the other in the Southern Hemisphere within the Antarctic Circle. One temperate zone lay in the Northern Hemisphere between the Arctic Circle and the Tropic of Cancer, the other in the Southern Hemisphere between the Antarctic Circle and the Tropic of Capricorn. The torrid zone straddled the Equator between the two tropics. While it accounted for latitude, however, this simple grouping of climates ignored other factors affecting temperature and climate.

The classification systems most widely used today are based on the one introduced in 1900 by the German climatologist Wladimir Köppen. Köppen divided Earth's surface into climatic regions that generally corresponded to patterns of vegetation and soils found throughout the world. The boundaries of these climatic regions were defined by using precise temperature and precipitation averages. A unique letter system identified five major climate groups—tropical rainy climates (A), dry climates (B), humid

WLADIMIR KÖPPEN

The German scientist Wladimir Köppen is known for his role in describing and mapping the climatic regions of the world. His achievements greatly influenced the study of climate, weather, and the atmosphere.

Wladimir Köppen was born on Sept. 25, 1846, in St. Petersburg, Russia. In 1864 he entered the University of St. Petersburg, where he specialized in botany. In 1867 he transferred to the University of Heidelberg in Germany where he studied the relation of plant growth to temperature. In the 1870s he was named head meteorologist at the German Naval Observatory in Hamburg, and in 1884 he produced a world map of temperature belts, ranging from polar to tropical latitudes.

A major achievement in climatology was reached in 1900 when Köppen introduced his mathematical system of climatic classification. Each of five major climate types was assigned a mathematical value according to temperature and rainfall. Since then, many of the systems introduced by other scholars have been based on Köppen's work.

Köppen retired from his position at the Hamburg observatory in 1919 and moved to Graz, Austria, in 1924. In 1927 he began editing, with Rudolph Geiger, a five-volume handbook of climatology. The work was nearly completed when Köppen died, on June 22, 1940.

moderate-temperature climates (C), humid low-temperature climates (D), and polar, snow climates (E). The climates were further subdivided by additional letters that referred to seasonal variations and extremes of precipitation and temperature.

A classification of climates introduced by the United States climatologist C. Warren Thornthwaite in 1931 divided the world into five vegetation-humidity zones—wet rainforest, humid forest, subhumid grassland, semiarid steppe, and arid desert—and into six vegetation-temperature zones—tropical, moderate temperature, low temperature, taiga, tundra, and frost. This book uses a modification of Köppen's classification, dividing the world into low-latitude, middle-latitude, and high-latitude climates, or into tropical, subtropical, cyclonic, and polar climates. Highland and oceanic climates are also discussed.

Each climate classification takes into account the relationship between temperature and precipitation effectiveness, in which the total amount of evaporation (moisture that is converted into vapor) is subtracted to determine the amount of precipitation actually available to support plant growth. In order to be classed as humid, for example,

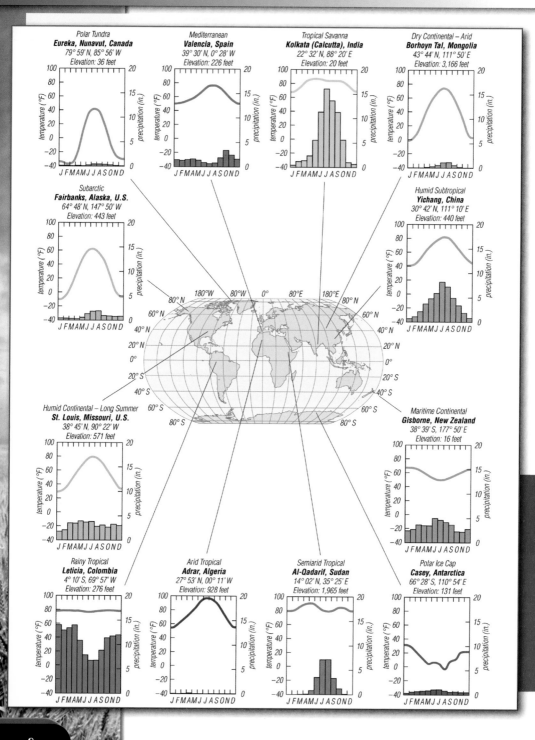

Polar Tundra
Eureka, Nunavut, Canada
79° 59' N, 85° 56' W
Elevation: 36 feet

Mediterranean
Valencia, Spain
39° 30' N, 0° 28' W
Elevation: 226 feet

Tropical Savanna
Kolkata (Calcutta), India
22° 32' N, 88° 20' E
Elevation: 20 feet

Dry Continental – Arid
Borhoyn Tal, Mongolia
43° 44' N, 111° 50' E
Elevation: 3,166 feet

Subarctic
Fairbanks, Alaska, U.S.
64° 48' N, 147° 50' W
Elevation: 443 feet

Humid Subtropical
Yichang, China
30° 42' N, 111° 10' E
Elevation: 440 feet

Humid Continental – Long Summer
St. Louis, Missouri, U.S.
38° 45' N, 90° 22' W
Elevation: 571 feet

Maritime Continental
Gisborne, New Zealand
38° 39' S, 177° 50' E
Elevation: 16 feet

Rainy Tropical
Leticia, Colombia
4° 10' S, 69° 57' W
Elevation: 276 feet

Arid Tropical
Adrar, Algeria
27° 53' N, 00° 11' W
Elevation: 928 feet

Semiarid Tropical
Al-Qadarif, Sudan
14° 02' N, 35° 25' E
Elevation: 1,965 feet

Polar Ice Cap
Casey, Antarctica
66° 28' S, 110° 54' E
Elevation: 131 feet

18

a region with high temperatures must have more precipitation than a region with low temperatures because its evaporation rates are greater. Thus a 10-inch (25-cm) average annual precipitation might well support a forest of coniferous trees (such as the evergreens spruce, fir, and pine) in a cool climate but only desert shrubs in a warm one.

Graphs show climate statistics for 12 cities with different climate types. The line graphs show mean monthly temperatures, corresponding to the scales at left, while the bar graphs below them show mean monthly precipitation levels, corresponding to the scales at right. The values are long-term averages calculated for the period 1961 to 1990. (To convert from degrees Fahrenheit to degrees Celsius, subtract 32 and then divide by 1.8. To convert from inches to centimeters, multiply by 2.54.) **Encyclopædia Britannica, Inc.**

Climate is determined by a variety of factors, called controls. Climate controls include latitude, land and water distribution, prevailing winds and belts of high and low pressure, ocean currents, altitude, topography, clouds, and cyclonic activity.

LATITUDE

Great amounts of energy are required for the massive movements of the air in the atmosphere and for the exchange of heat and moisture between the atmosphere and Earth's land and water surfaces that are the essence of weather and climate. This energy comes from the Sun. Incoming solar radiation, or insolation, is not evenly distributed. Much more is received in the low latitudes, near the Equator, than in the high latitudes, near the poles. This is mainly because latitude, the primary control of climate, determines the angle at which the Sun's rays strike Earth's surface. Latitude also determines the length of daylight, or the time during which solar energy reaches Earth at any angle.

Only in the tropics—those areas around the Equator between 23.5° N latitude (the Tropic of Cancer) and 23.5° S latitude (the Tropic of Capricorn)—does the Sun ever appear directly overhead. For that reason, only those areas ever receive the rays of the Sun vertically (at an angle of 90°). The average angle of the Sun's rays decreases toward the poles. As a result, the solar energy is spread over a greater area at high latitudes than at low latitudes, and less solar energy reaches Earth's surface at high latitudes because more is absorbed and reflected by the atmosphere.

The length of daylight is about 12 hours everywhere on Earth at the time of the equinoxes (about March 21 and September 23). This is not the case year-round, however, because Earth's spin axis is tilted. The length of daylight is always about 12 hours at the Equator but increases toward each pole in summer, reaching a maximum at the time of the summer solstice (about June 21 in the Northern Hemisphere and about December 21 in the Southern Hemisphere). Likewise, the length of daylight decreases toward each pole in winter, reaching a minimum at the winter solstice (about December 21 in the Northern Hemisphere and about June 21 in the Southern Hemisphere).

The area on Earth where the Sun appears directly overhead at noon shifts north and south as the planet orbits the Sun, reaching the Tropic of Cancer at the June solstice and the Tropic of Capricorn at the December solstice. The zone of maximum insolation swings back and forth over the Equator along with the area where the Sun is directly overhead. Because of the additional heating from

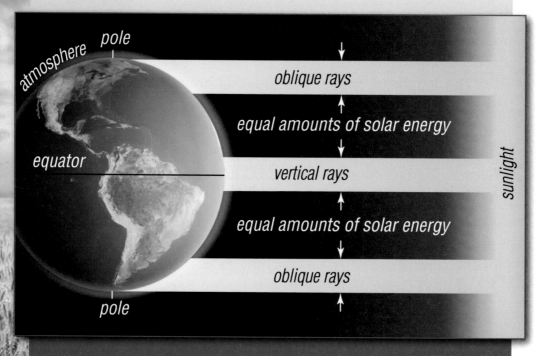

atmosphere · pole

oblique rays

equal amounts of solar energy

equator

vertical rays

sunlight

equal amounts of solar energy

oblique rays

pole

Energy received from the Sun is greater near the Equator than near the poles because the Sun's rays are more concentrated at the Equator and pass through less of the atmosphere. **Encyclopædia Britannica, Inc.**

the longer periods of daylight toward the poles in summer, however, the zone of maximum insolation moves beyond the tropics to between 30° and 40° N latitude in July and 30° and 40° S latitude in January.

In the lower latitudes, Earth gains more heat by radiation from the Sun than it loses to space by radiation from Earth. In the higher latitudes, Earth gives off more heat than it receives from the Sun. This unequal heating and cooling would result in ever-increasing temperatures in the tropics and

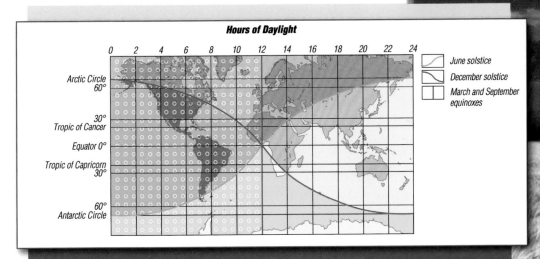

Hours of Daylight

The length of daylight varies by latitude and by time of year. At 30° N latitude, for example, daylight is 14 hours long in June and 10 hours long in December. At 60° N latitude, daylight lasts for more than 18 hours in June but for less than 6 hours in December. At the Equator there are always 12 hours of daylight. **Encyclopædia Britannica, Inc.**

ever-decreasing temperatures in the polar regions if it were not for the continuous transfer of heat from low latitudes to high latitudes by winds and ocean currents.

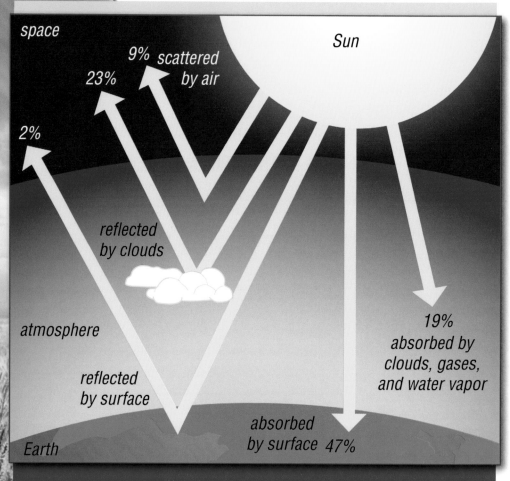

space

Sun

9% *scattered*
by air

23%

2%

reflected
by clouds

atmosphere

19%
absorbed by
clouds, gases,
and water vapor

reflected
by surface

absorbed
by surface 47%

Earth

Earth absorbs about 47 percent of total insolation, and the atmosphere about 19 percent. About 34 percent is reflected back into space—23 percent by clouds, 9 percent by the atmosphere, and 2 percent by Earth's surface. **Encyclopædia Britannica, Inc.**

LAND AND WATER DISTRIBUTION

The irregular distribution of land and water surfaces is a major control of climate. Air temperatures are warmer in summer and colder in winter over the continents than they are over the oceans at the same latitude. This is because landmasses heat and cool more rapidly than bodies of water do. Bodies of water thus tend to moderate the air temperatures over nearby land areas, warming them in winter and cooling them in summer. The interiors of large landmasses such as Eurasia (Europe and Asia) are affected least by the oceans and so have greater annual temperature ranges than do coastal areas and the interiors of small landmasses. Large permanent ice surfaces reflect away most of the Sun's energy and then affect climate by chilling the air over them and the land and water surrounding them.

PREVAILING WINDS AND PRESSURE BELTS

Prevailing winds and pressure belts are major climate controls. A belt of low pressure known as the intertropical convergence zone (ITCZ) lies along the Equator. On either side of the equatorial low, between 25° and 30° latitude

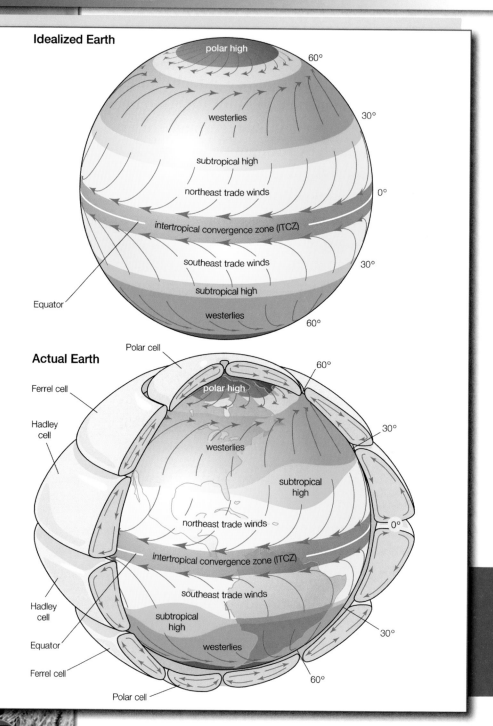

Idealized Earth

polar high

60°

westerlies

30°

subtropical high

northeast trade winds

0°

intertropical convergence zone (ITCZ)

southeast trade winds

30°

subtropical high

Equator

westerlies

60°

Actual Earth

Polar cell

Ferrel cell

Hadley cell

60°

polar high

30°

westerlies

subtropical high

northeast trade winds

0°

intertropical convergence zone (ITCZ)

southeast trade winds

Hadley cell

subtropical high

30°

Equator

westerlies

Ferrel cell

60°

Polar cell

in each hemisphere, is a belt of high-pressure centers over the oceans. From the equatorial side of these subtropical highs—such as the Hawaiian high over the North Pacific—blow the warm, moist tropical easterlies (winds blowing from east to west), or trade winds.

From the polar side of the subtropical highs, to about 60° latitude in each hemisphere, blow the moist but cooler prevailing westerlies. At about 60° latitude are belts of low pressure, with centers over the oceans. Into these subpolar lows—such as the Aleutian low over the North Pacific—blow not only the westerlies but also cold easterly winds from polar high-pressure centers located over the Arctic Ocean and Antarctica.

The pressure and wind belts shift along with the area where the Sun appears directly overhead at noon—to the north when the Northern Hemisphere has its summer and to the south when the Southern Hemisphere has its summer. As is true with temperature patterns, the east-west alignment of pressure

General patterns of atmospheric circulation are shown over an idealized Earth with a uniform surface (top) and the actual Earth (bottom). Both horizontal and vertical patterns of atmospheric circulation are depicted on the diagram of the actual Earth. **Encyclopædia Britannica, Inc.**

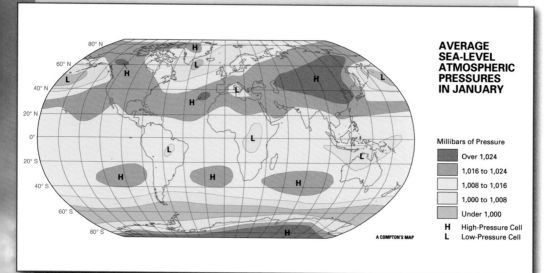

The map shows global mean air pressure at sea level in January.

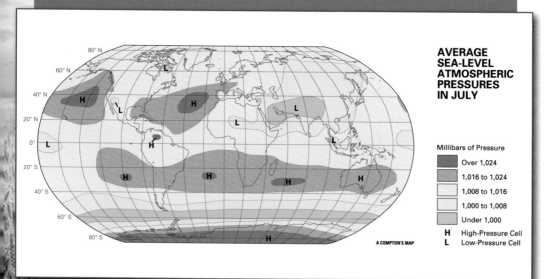

The map shows global mean air pressure at sea level in July.

patterns is greatly modified by the arrangement of the world's landmasses and oceans. Most notable are the intense winter high over northern Asia and the summer low over southwestern Asia. These pressure centers are major influences on the monsoon winds that blow out of Asia in the winter and into it in the summer.

OCEAN CURRENTS

The major ocean currents also are a climate control. They follow the prevailing winds that circle the oceanic subtropical highs—clockwise in the Northern Hemisphere and counterclockwise in the Southern Hemisphere. Wherever these currents flow toward the polar regions—on the western sides of the lows—they carry warm water away from the equatorial regions. Where they flow toward the Equator—on the eastern sides of the lows—they carry cold water from the polar regions. Ocean currents such as the Gulf Stream and the North Atlantic Current carry warm water northward and eastward around the Azores high, which moderates the climate of western Europe. There are similar warm currents around the

Hawaiian high in the North Pacific and around the highs in the South Atlantic, South Pacific, and Indian oceans.

ALTITUDE

Another climate control is altitude, or elevation. Just as there is a gradual decrease in average temperature with increasing latitude, there is a decrease in temperature with increasing elevation. High mountains near the Equator, for example, may have tropical vegetation at their bases but permanent ice and snow at their summits. The reasons for this are somewhat different for mountains as opposed to wide, elevated areas, such as plateaus. Mountains are exposed to atmosphere that is far above the surrounding lowlands. This air receives little heat from the ground far below, so that it is colder by about 3.6 °F for every 1,000 foot increase in elevation (about 6.5 °C per 1,000 meters). Plateaus are effectively "on the ground," but there is less air above to trap heat, so that such places are about 2.4 °F cooler per 1,000 feet (4.4 °C per 1,000 meters) in elevation than they would be otherwise. Temperatures cited later in this book should be considered sea-level equivalents, unless otherwise indicated.

RELIEF

The topography, or relief, of land has an important effect on climate. Windward mountain slopes, facing moisture-bearing winds, usually receive more precipitation than do either the lower, more level mountain bases or the mountain slopes in the lee (the sheltered side) of the winds. This is because air moving up a mountain slope expands and cools, reducing the amount of moisture needed for saturation (the state in which no more water vapor can be in the air under those conditions). Condensation, clouds, and precipitation are thus frequently produced. Air moving down a mountain slope compresses and warms, increasing the amount of moisture possible in the air, and thus reducing the likelihood of precipitation. This helps explain why the coast of the U.S. states of Oregon and Washington has heavy precipitation while the interior generally has a dry climate.

Mountain ranges may also serve as barriers to outbreaks of cold air. In this way the Alps and other mountain ranges of southern Europe protect much of the Mediterranean coast. Similarly the Himalayas protect the lowlands of India.

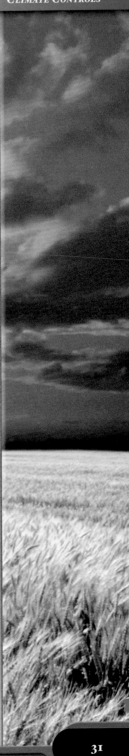

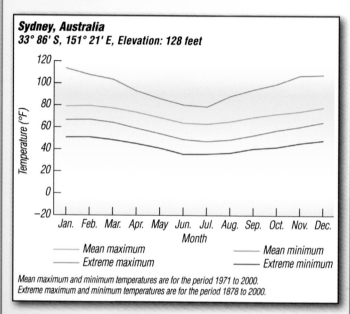

COMPARING CLIMATES

Sydney, Australia
33° 86' S, 151° 21' E, Elevation: 128 feet

——— Mean maximum   ——— Mean minimum
——— Extreme maximum   ——— Extreme minimum

Mean maximum and minimum temperatures are for the period 1971 to 2000.
Extreme maximum and minimum temperatures are for the period 1878 to 2000.

Long-term temperature data for Sydney, Australia, show that the city has mild winters and warm summers and that temperature extremes are more variable in the summer. Encyclopædia Britannica, Inc.

It is interesting to compare the climates of places that have much in common and yet certain different characteristics, to illustrate the effects of some of the controls of climate. As an example, consider Sydney, in southeastern Australia, and Atlanta, in the southeastern United States. Both are 34 °From the Equator, though in opposite hemispheres. As a result, both have about the same mean annual

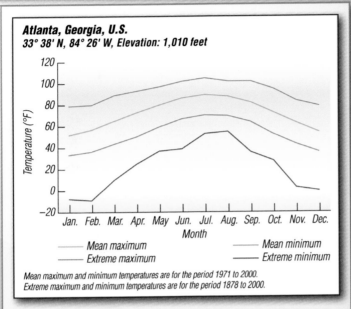

Atlanta, Georgia, U.S.
33° 38' N, 84° 26' W, Elevation: 1,010 feet

Temperature (°F)

Month

Mean maximum   Mean minimum
Extreme maximum   Extreme minimum

Mean maximum and minimum temperatures are for the period 1971 to 2000.
Extreme maximum and minimum temperatures are for the period 1878 to 2000.

Atlanta, Georgia, has cool winters and hot summers, and temperatures vary more in the winter. **Encyclopædia Britannica, Inc.**

temperature—65 °F (18 °C) for Sydney and 62 °F (17 °C) for Atlanta—with the small difference due mainly to Atlanta's elevation being nearly 1,000 feet (300 meters) higher. (The temperatures given in this section are not sea-level equivalents.) However, Sydney's coldest month, July, at 55 °F (13 °C), is much warmer than Atlanta's coldest month, January, at 43 °F (6 °C). Sydney's warmest month, February, at 73 °F (23 °C), is cooler than Atlanta's warmest month, July, at 80 °F (27 °C). Much of this difference is due to Sydney's almost immediate coastal location, while Atlanta is about

200 miles (320 km) from the nearest water. It is also partly due to Australia being smaller than North America, thus allowing more of a maritime influence.

Extreme temperatures further illustrate differences between the two locations. Atlanta, with land poleward all the way to the Canadian Arctic, has (rarely) seen temperatures as low as −9 °F (−23 °C). Sydney, with a great expanse of open sea poleward between Australia and Antarctica, never drops below 35 °F (2 °C), though it gets almost that cold fairly often. On the other hand, Atlanta's highest recorded temperature, which has been nearly equaled on several occasions, is 105 °F (41 °C), but Sydney has (rarely) soared to 114 °F (46 °C) when air has arrived from the hot tropical interior of Australia. In short, Atlanta has cool, quite variable winters and hot, monotonous summers, while Sydney has mild, relatively monotonous winters and warm, but potentially quite variable summers. Thus, there is much more to climate than mere averages.

CLOUDS

Clouds exert a significant effect on climate; they are generally associated with humid environments. Temperatures tend to be less extreme in areas with heavy cloud cover. During daylight and in summer, clouds keep temperatures from rising as high as they otherwise might by reducing the amount of heat received from the Sun. At night and in winter, clouds keep temperatures from falling as much as they otherwise might by reducing the amount of heat radiated into space.

CYCLONIC ACTIVITY

Traveling low-pressure centers known as frontal or wave cyclones generally move from west to east and are associated with the systems of cold and warm fronts that produce the variable weather of the middle and higher latitudes. Wave cyclones form along the undulating boundary, or "front," between cold polar air masses and warm tropical air masses. They are stronger in winter, when temperature contrasts in the frontal zones are greater.

CHAPTER 3
TROPICAL AND SUBTROPICAL CLIMATES

The tropical climates lie in the low latitudes and are dominated by tropical and equatorial air masses. They are warm all year with at most a minor cool season. The area between 20° and 40° latitude is considered subtropical and can be further distinguished by the level of humidity typically found there. The dry subtropical and so-called Mediterranean climates are generally found poleward from the dry tropics.

TROPICAL RAINFOREST

In areas with rainy tropical, or tropical rainforest climates, precipitation is heavy, usually averaging more than 80 inches (200 cm) per year. Humidity is high, and thunderstorms occur almost every day. Every month has a mean temperature close to 80 °F (27 °C). Temperature variations are small, so that many such locations never experience high temperatures over 100 °F (38 °C) or lows below 60 °F (16 °C). Vegetation consists of

With abundant rainfall and warm temperatures year-round, a tropical rainforest in Ecuador is lush with vegetation. © Victor Englebert

dense rainforests of broad-leaved evergreen trees. Poorly drained areas have mangrove swamps. Where tree cover is thin and sunlight reaches the ground, there is dense undergrowth known as jungle.

Rainy tropical climates generally occur in the equatorial lowlands and along mountainous tropical coasts exposed to the moist easterly trade winds. The Amazon Basin in

AMAZON RAINFOREST

Boat traffic on the Amazon River near Gurupá, Pará state, Brazil. © Elizabeth Harris/Tony Stone Images

The world's largest continuous tropical rainforest occupies the region surrounding the Amazon River in northern South America. The Amazon Rainforest stretches from the Atlantic Ocean in the east to the Andes Mountains in the west. It makes up about 40 percent of Brazil's total area.

The huge extent of the Amazon Rainforest is a reflection of the warm, rainy, and humid climate. The lengths of day and night are equal on the Equator, which runs slightly north of the river. The usually clear nights allow the heat received from the Sun during the 12-hour day to radiate fairly rapidly back into the atmosphere. There is a greater temperature difference between daytime and midnight than between the warmest and coolest months. Thus, night can be considered the winter of the Amazon. The average daily temperature at Manaus, a Brazilian city at the heart of the rainforest, is in the upper 80s °F (about 32 °C) in September and the mid-70s °F (about 24 °C) in April. However, the humidity is consistently high and often oppressive.

Rainfall in the lowlands typically ranges from 60 to 120 inches (150 to 300 mm) annually in the central Amazon region (for example, Manaus). In the central area there is a dry period, usually from June to November. Manaus has experienced as many as 60 consecutive days without rain. On the eastern and northwestern edges of the region, however, rainfall occurs year-round. The highest amounts of rainfall, up to 140 inches (350 mm), are recorded along the Putumayo River, a tributary of the Amazon, in southern Colombia.

The remarkably rich and diverse plant and animal life of the Amazon region is a resource of world importance. The forest contains several million species of insects, plants, birds, fish, and other forms of life, many still unrecorded by science.

South America and the Congo Basin in Africa are the largest continuous areas that have a rainy tropical climate. Other areas are in the islands of Southeast Asia, the eastern coast of Madagascar, and the windward coasts of Central America.

TROPICAL SAVANNA

On the poleward side of the rainy tropics, generally between about 5° and 20° latitude, lie the wet-and-dry tropics, which have a tropical savanna climate. Precipitation is not as heavy as in the tropics, and there is a long dry season, mainly in "winter" when the Sun is lower in the sky. As a result, the vegetation is typically tall grasses and scattered trees. The highest mean monthly temperatures, usually just before the rainy season, may be in the 90s °F (30s °C). Principal areas with a tropical savanna climate are in Central America, South America, Africa, India, Southeast Asia, and Australia.

TROPICAL STEPPE

The dry season is longer and the wet season is shorter toward the poleward edges of the tropical savanna, where it merges with the tropical steppe, which has a semiarid tropical climate. Farther poleward, generally between 15° and 30° latitude, the steppe merges with the tropical desert, which has an arid tropical climate. Average annual precipitation generally is less than 30 inches (76 cm) in the tropical steppe and less than 10 inches (25 cm) in the tropical desert. In both these regions, mean monthly temperatures in the summer may reach well into the 90s °F (30s °C). Temperatures in the tropical deserts are the highest in the world, with extreme afternoon highs of more than 130 °F (54 °C). Only short grasses and desert shrubs survive there.

TROPICAL DESERT

The principal tropical deserts are the Sahara and the Kalahari in Africa, the Sonoran in northern Mexico and the southwestern United States, those of Australia, and those of Arabia, Iran, and Pakistan in southwestern Asia. The tropical deserts on continental western coasts result from the influence of the cool ocean currents and dry winds on the eastern sides of the oceanic subtropical high-pressure centers. Examples are the Namib in southwestern Africa, the Atacama in Chile, and those along the coasts of Baja California and Morocco.

One of the driest areas in the world, the Rub' al-Khali is a vast tropical desert that lies mostly within Saudi Arabia. Vegetation is very scarce there. **Lynn Abercrombie**

MEDITERRANEAN SUBTROPICAL

The Mediterranean climate is distinguished by warm to hot, dry summers and cool to mild, fairly wet winters. Areas with this climate generally lie on west-facing coasts at latitudes between about 30° and 40°. There are Mediterranean climates on the coasts of southern California and central Chile, on the Mediterranean coasts of southern Europe and northern Africa, and along parts of the southern coasts of Africa and Australia. Summers typically have mean temperatures near 80 °F (27 °C), and winters average around 50 °F (10 °C), with occasional freezing

The coast of Sousse, Tunisia, like much of northern Africa, is characterized by a Mediterranean climate. Shutterstock.com

temperatures. Average annual precipitation ranges from less than 15 inches (38 cm) on the equatorial side, where the Mediterranean climate region merges with dry regions, to 35 to 40 inches (89 to 101 cm) on the poleward side.

DRY SUBTROPICAL

Dry subtropical climates exist in such places as central Spain, the Middle East, South Africa, and the interior of eastern Australia. Temperatures are slightly warmer than those of the Mediterranean climate, and winter rains are reduced, often by the greater distance from water.

HUMID SUBTROPICAL

The humid subtropical climate is generally located between 25° and 35° latitude on the east sides of continents. It is primarily influenced by the warm maritime tropical air masses on the west sides of the subtropical oceanic high-pressure centers. Precipitation, from thunderstorms in summer and cyclonic storms in winter, is moderate and year-round. It averages between 30 and 60 inches (76 and 152 cm) per year, enough for the growth of forests. Winters are short and mild, with mean

temperatures in the 40s° or 50s °F (5° to 15 °C), but temperatures fall below freezing during occasional invasions of polar air. The summer months have mean temperatures in the low 80s °F (about 28 °C). Humid subtropical climates are found in the southeastern United States, southeastern China and southern Japan, in the southern Brazil–Uruguay–northeastern Argentina area, and along the southeastern coasts of Africa and Australia.

CHAPTER 4
CYCLONIC CLIMATES

Dominated by the conflict between cold polar and warm tropical air masses and by the movement of frontal cyclones, the cyclonic climate regions lie in a broad belt between 35° and 70° latitude. Cyclonic climates, at least as experienced on land, are overwhelmingly confined to the Northern Hemisphere, where the landmasses are much larger and extend much farther into the middle and upper latitudes than they do in the Southern Hemisphere. The cyclonic climates can be subdivided into humid continental; subarctic, or taiga; dry continental; and maritime continental.

HUMID CONTINENTAL

Humid continental cyclonic climates are found in the northeastern and north-central United States and southeastern Canada; northeastern China; northern Japan; Azerbaijan, Armenia, and Georgia; parts of Central Asia and Russia; and eastern and central Europe. Summers are longest and warmest toward the Equator, while winters are longest and

Satellite image of Hurricane Humberto, which passed close to Bermuda in September 2001 but did not cause any damage. Cyclones that form in the North Atlantic Ocean are known as hurricanes. **NASA Goddard Space Flight Center**

coldest toward the poles. Mean monthly temperatures in the north range from the upper 60s °F (about 20 °C) in the summer to below 0 °F (-18 °C) in the winter. In the south they range between the upper 70s °F (about 26 °C) in the summer and the lower 30s °F (around 0 °C) in the winter.

Precipitation, from both thunderstorms and cyclonic storms, occurs year-round but usually with a summer maximum. The annual average varies between 25 and 60 inches (63 and 152 cm). Snow is common, especially in the north. Native vegetation varies from tall prairie grasses in the drier margins to forests of deciduous trees (trees that lose their leaves each fall) in the south and those of coniferous trees in the north.

SUBARCTIC

The subarctic cyclonic climate region, or taiga, lies to the north of the humid continental climate regions, between 50° and 70° N latitude. It covers much of Alaska and northern Canada in North America and much of Scandinavia, Russia, the Baltic countries, Belarus, and Manchuria in Eurasia. In these areas are the source regions of the cold continental polar air masses.

Summers are short and cool—only three months of the year average more than 50 °F (10 °C). During summer there are occasional

The taiga, or boreal forest, in Alaska exhibits its many autumn colors. Shutterstock.com

nighttime frosts, though temperatures rise into the 70s °F (20s °C) during daylight. Winters are long and bitterly cold, with mean January temperatures far below 0 °F (- 18 °C). In northeastern Siberia, minimum temperatures of - 90 °F (- 67 °C) have been recorded. The ranges between the January and July mean temperatures reach more than 100 °F (56 °C), greater than anywhere else in the world.

Precipitation usually averages less than 20 inches (50 cm) per year. It is mostly from year-round cyclonic storms, with a maximum during the summer rains. Winter snowfalls are only a small portion of the total precipitation, but snow covers the ground for most of the year. There are large areas of permanently frozen subsoil, or permafrost. The subarctic climate generally coincides with a broad belt of coniferous trees known as the boreal forest or taiga.

DRY CONTINENTAL

The dry continental cyclonic climates occur between 35° and 50° latitude, lying either in the lee of mountains or far inland. The three main areas of dry continental climate are the Great Plains and Great Basin of North

TAIGA

The taiga, or boreal forest, covers most of the subarctic climate region. It extends in a belt across North America, Europe, and Asia between the latitudes 60° N and 50° N. The

The moose is one of many animals to make its home in the taiga. **Eastcott Momatiuk/Lifesize/ Getty Images**

taiga lies south of the frigid region called the tundra. The taiga is warmer than the tundra and also receives more precipitation, mostly in summer. The winters are long and cold, while the summers are short and cool to moderately warm.

Climate is the most important environmental factor affecting the distribution of plant and animal species. Suitable conditions of temperature and moisture are vital to all organisms. The taiga, with a milder climate than the tundra, also has greater diversity of plant and animal life. However, the taiga has less diversity than warmer zones to the south.

Evergreen conifers — needle-leaved shrubs and trees such as pines, firs, and spruces — dominate the taiga. Some areas have hardwoods, such as birch and aspen, that are deciduous, meaning that they lose and regrow their leaves seasonally. Many areas of the taiga have dense stands of a few species of tree. As a result of their thick growth, little light reaches the lower levels of the forest and fewer plants grow there. Animals of the taiga include bears, moose, wolves, lynx, reindeer, shrews, snowshoe hares, and rodents.

America; Mongolia, northwestern China, and parts of Central Asia; and northwestern and southern Argentina in South America. Toward the Equator, they merge with the dry subtropical and arid tropical regions and are distinguished mainly by their lower winter temperatures. Summers are hot, with mean temperatures in some places rising above 80 °F (27 °C). Precipitation is low and variable, especially in the areas with the dry continental–arid (desert) climate.

Sand dunes in California's Death Valley. Stockbyte/Thinkstock

Annual precipitation in midlatitude deserts such as Death Valley in California and the Taklimakan, the Gobi, and the area around the Aral Sea in Asia averages less than 5 inches (13 cm). The semiarid steppes around these deserts average up to 20 inches (50 cm) or more.

MARITIME CONTINENTAL

The maritime continental cyclonic climate occurs on the western coasts of the continents between about 35° and 60° latitude. It is also often referred to as the temperate maritime or marine west coast climate. On the equatorial side it merges with the Mediterranean climate. Areas with maritime continental climate are on the Pacific coast of North America from southeastern Alaska to northern California; on the Pacific coast of South America in southern Chile; in northwestern Europe, from Norway and Iceland to Portugal; and in New Zealand and southeastern Australia.

Temperatures are moderated by the prevailing westerly winds moving onshore from the oceanic high-pressure centers. Winters are mild, with mean temperatures in the 40s° or 50s °F (5° to 15 °C). Summers also are mild, with means in the 60s °F (10s °C). Temperatures seldom fall below 20 °F (- 7 °C) in winter or rise above 85° F (30 °C) in summer. Average annual precipitation varies from 20 or 30 inches (50 to 76 cm) in low-lying areas and at the equatorial margins to more than 100 inches (250 cm) on windward mountain slopes. Precipitation occurs year-round but is much greater in winter, when cyclonic storm activity increases. Winter fog is common. Where precipitation is heavy, there often are dense forests of coniferous trees.

CHAPTER 5

OTHER TYPES
OF CLIMATE

Tropical, subtropical, and cyclonic climates cover most parts of the world where people live. However, other climate types prevail in certain areas. Harsh polar climates are controlled by the polar and arctic air masses of high latitudes (60° N and S and higher). Highland climates can be found at any latitude; the primary factor influencing this climate type is altitude. Oceanic climates are found on small islands and out at sea.

POLAR CLIMATES

The polar tundra climate is found just poleward of the subarctic climate, mainly beyond the Arctic Circle on the northern fringes of North America and Eurasia. Winters in the tundra, as in the subarctic, are long and bitterly cold, with temperatures often dropping to - 70 °F (- 57 °C). There is no true summer. Temperatures seldom rise above 60 °F (15 °C), and usually only two or three months have

Pool located on Canada's Ellesmere Island in the tundra. **Doug Allan/ The Image Bank/Getty Images**

mean temperatures above freezing. Annual precipitation, mostly from cyclonic summer storms, usually averages less than 15 inches (38 cm). There are no trees, and permafrost underlies the soil.

The polar ice cap climate has no month with a mean temperature above freezing. Almost all of Antarctica and all but the coast of Greenland have this coldest of all climates.

TUNDRA

The huge plain called the tundra covers much of the land between the North Pole and the taiga, in some places farther south than latitude 60° N. This region is so cold that a layer of permanently frozen soil, called permafrost, lies under the rocky topsoil. Although the tundra receives little precipitation, bogs and ponds often form, because little evaporation and drainage take place.

The number of plant and animal species in the tundra is low compared to other regions. Life abounds during the warmer months, but only species specially adapted to the long frozen winters can survive year-round. In the winter most of the organisms become dormant or migrate to warmer regions. Lichens, mosses, and grasses are the dominant ground cover, but some flowering plants are abundant during the short, cool summers. There are some low and dwarf shrubs but no trees. Animals include wolves, foxes, reindeer (caribou), voles, squirrels, and hares, as well as birds, insects, and fish. Amphibians and reptiles are rare.

These areas are covered by permanent snow and ice and some bare rock. There is no vegetation. Winter temperatures are most extreme in the interior of Antarctica, reaching world record lows of less than - 125 °F (- 87 °C)—partly from the high altitude of the ice cap, which reaches elevations of over 11,000 feet (3,350 meters) in some spots. Even in the summer months temperatures barely rise above freezing and often drop far below 0 °F (- 18 °C). Average annual precipitation—mostly snow—is usually less than 5 inches (13 cm).

HIGHLAND CLIMATES

Highlands are generally cooler than lowlands of the same latitude. Precipitation is much greater on the lower, windward mountain slopes than it is at higher elevations and on the leeward slopes. Great heights often have permanent snow cover. The snow line, or upper limit of summertime melting (for example, the lower edge of a mountaintop snowcap), is generally highest in the tropics and lowest at high latitudes. The most extensive highland areas are the Rocky Mountains of North America, the

Andes Mountains of South America, and the Himalayan mountain–Tibetan plateau area of Asia. Mountain climates are often similar to those near sea level much farther from the Equator. For example, above about 6,000

The snow-covered Shivling mountain in the Himalayas is subject to a cold highland climate. Shutterstock.com

feet (1,800 meters) the mountains in North Carolina and Tennessee have about the same temperature and vegetation as low-lying areas in eastern Canada, about 700 miles (1,100 km) to the north.

OCEANIC CLIMATES

People living on small islands or traveling by ship experience climates dominated by the strong moderating influence of large bodies of water. Mean annual temperatures are often similar to those at the same latitude over continents, but the range of temperature is much smaller. For example, the Azores islands, at 39° N latitude in the eastern Atlantic, have a mean temperature in the coldest months (February and March) of about 57 °F (14 °C), yet the warmest month (August) is not much warmer, averaging 71 °F (22 °C).

Rain falls on the oceans, with less obvious effects than on land. Subtropical areas generally get less rain than equatorial or mid-latitude places. Some oceanic areas are quite stormy. The seas surrounding Antarctica have frequent cyclonic storms with strong winds and large waves. Tropical oceans often experience tropical storms and tropical cyclones

Women stand in the debris left in a village east of Manila after it was hit by Typhoon Ketsana. Ketsana was a tropical storm that devastated parts of the Philippines and much of Southeast Asia when it struck the region in September 2009. **Ted Aljibe/AFP/Getty Images**

(also called hurricanes or typhoons) in that hemisphere's late summer and autumn. Such storms often strike land, with potentially devastating results.

CHAPTER 6
THE EFFECTS
OF CLIMATE

The impact of climate is far-reaching, affecting everything from the survival of the smallest organisms to decisions on where to build cities and towns. Climate is both a part of, and a dominant influence on, a region's natural environment. It affects not only a region's life-forms but also the land itself. The many basic human activities that are largely dependent on climate include agriculture and transportation.

CLIMATE AND THE NATURAL ENVIRONMENT

Of all aspects of the natural landscape, none is affected to a greater degree by climate than is natural vegetation. Each plant species survives only within certain limits of sunlight, temperature, precipitation, humidity, soil moisture, and wind. Variations in these elements are directly reflected in variations in Earth's plant cover. The correspondence between climate and vegetation is so apparent that climate types often are identical with and are given the same names as the dominant natural vegetation in a region, as is the case with the taiga and the tundra.

Climate also affects soils. In warm, wet climates, weathering and formation of soil are more rapid than in cool, dry climates. As a result, soils are generally thicker in the wet tropics than in deserts or polar forest areas. Soils in dry climates, however, tend to be more fertile than those in humid climates. This is mainly because there is less leaching, or removal of plant nutrients from the soil by the downward percolation (seepage) of water. Soil composition also depends on the effect that climate has in determining the type of vegetation that eventually decays and becomes part of the soil. That is why grassland soils are more fertile than forest soils.

Variations in climate likewise have a marked effect on Earth's landforms. In humid areas, where water is the chief erosional force, landforms tend to have rounded contours. Landforms shaped under arid conditions are more likely to be jagged and angular. This is partly because wind erosion is more dominant. Stream erosion in dry areas, while infrequent, tends to be sudden

The distinctive sandstone formations of the Bungle Bungle Range in Australia's Purnululu National Park were largely shaped by erosion. Sam Abell/National Geographic Image Collection/Getty Images

and torrential, and the runoff of water is not slowed down as much by plant cover.

CLIMATE AND HUMANS

As part of the natural environment, climate greatly affects human activities. Climate is economically most significant in its effect on agriculture. Climatic factors such as the

Traffic is often adversely affected in areas that experience severe climatic conditions, such as heavy snowfall. © www.istockphoto.com/ **Bill Grove**

length of growing season, the total amount and seasonal distribution of precipitation, and the daily and seasonal ranges of temperature restrict the kinds of crops and the types of livestock that can be raised.

People have reduced and even overcome climatic restrictions by the use of irrigation in dry climates, drainage in wet climates, and greenhouses in cold climates. New breeds

IRRIGATION

The green irrigated fields at an oasis in south-eastern Libya contrast sharply with the dry natural landscape behind them. **Derek Bayes/ Tony Stone Images**

Irrigation is the artificial supply of water to agricultural land. It is practiced by more than half the farmers in the world because they need more water for their crops than is available from rainfall. Modern irrigation, together with the application of fertilizers and mechanization, has resulted in an unprecedented increase in farm productivity.

Irrigation is required in crop raising wherever precipitation, both rainfall and snow,

amounts to less than 10 inches (25 cm) a year. In regions with an annual precipitation of only 10 to 20 inches (25 to 50 cm), some crops may be grown by dry-farming methods, but larger and more dependable yields can be obtained through irrigation. Even in regions with adequate annual rainfall, irrigation may be necessary if the seasonal distribution is such that a dry period comes during the growing season. This occurs in areas that have the so-called Mediterranean climate—as in southern California and much of Italy—in which winters are rainy and summers dry. In parts of India and China, heavy monsoon rains fall in summer, but crops grown before the rains begin each year must be irrigated.

In an irrigation system, water is pumped from natural ponds, lakes, streams, and wells. Basin systems and dams hold back larger streams and annual floods. Below the dam, gates are opened to concrete-lined canals, which carry the water over the land through gravity flow. More elaborate, expensive canals flow from huge constructed reservoirs, which hold a year-round water supply. Today, portable irrigation systems of lightweight aluminum pipe are widely used. Drip irrigation, a newer method, uses narrow tubing to supply water directly to the base of each plant.

of plants and animals, able to thrive under otherwise adverse climatic conditions, have been developed also. The grazing of livestock, however, still is largely limited to areas where forage crops—those cultivated mainly to feed livestock—can be profitably grown. Open-range grazing is particularly sensitive to climate, requiring relatively mild temperatures and adequate water supplies.

Climatic conditions also affect transportation. In areas of frequent storms and recurring fog, transportation movements are frequently slowed or interrupted. Water transportation in many areas is halted by winter ice. Land transportation may be blocked by heavy snowfalls. Air travel especially is affected by stormy climatic conditions.

The major concentrations of population in the world are in the humid middle latitudes and subtropics, where the development of agriculture has been least restricted by adverse climatic conditions. Areas with very dry, very wet, or very cold climates tend to be sparsely populated. However, with technological developments such as refrigeration, air conditioning, and central heating, human settlement has been less and less confined to so-called favorable climates.

While "climate" is intended as a long-term description of weather, there remains the question of just how long a period it should describe. If one adopts a period such as 30 years, one can then describe changes in climate over longer periods, such as thousands or millions of years. Evidence of climate changes includes data from rocks and fossils, tree rings, and lake bed sediments, and human historical records.

These changes have many causes which operate on many time scales. The drift of continents due to plate tectonics is an important factor over millions of years. Changes in Earth's orbit and axial tilt are a factor over tens of thousands of years. Varying levels of greenhouse gases, such as carbon dioxide, are important on both long and short time scales. These gases allow sunlight to pass through and warm Earth's surface but impede the flow of infrared energy back into space, thus "trapping" heat and warming the planet.

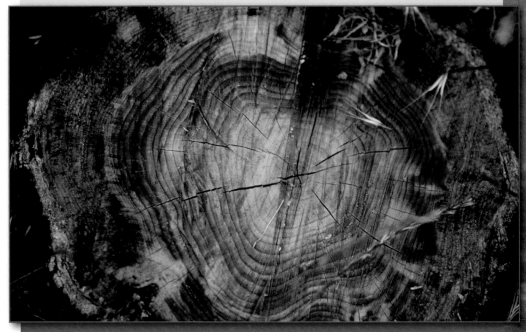

Tree rings, such as the ones shown here, provide evidence that climate change has occurred over time. **Pete Turner/Stone/Getty Images**

CLIMATE OVER TIME

In one sense, Earth's overall climate has been rather stable over most of its 4.5-billion-year history—at least enough to have allowed life to persist. While the Sun is believed to have grown about 50 percent brighter during this time, decreasing amounts of greenhouse gases in the past helped keep temperatures from rising much. However, quite different conditions

The Hubbard Glacier in Alaska. Shutterstock.com

have prevailed at times. For example, there is some evidence that ice may have covered almost the entire planet about 700 million years ago. On the other hand, much of the last 250 million years was quite warm, peaking around 55 million years ago. At that time there was no polar ice and the conditions now called tropical extended almost to the polar regions. After that, worldwide temperatures gradually cooled, eventually resulting in Antarctica and Greenland becoming ice covered.

ICE AGES AND INTERGLACIAL PERIODS

The last two million years have been a remarkable time of alternating ice ages and somewhat shorter warmer periods called interglacials. The current interglacial, called the Holocene epoch, began a bit more than 10,000 years ago. There have been variations even during the Holocene, including a period around 8,000 years ago when what is now the Sahara was relatively wet and green. In historic times, the period from about AD 1600 through much of the 1800s is known as the Little Ice Age, during which temperatures were a bit cooler than today and glaciers were generally growing.

CONCLUSION

Climate is incredibly varied across the globe and can impact life in a number of ways. There is currently widespread concern about a rapid phase of climate change, commonly known as global warming. While many complex factors, including slight variations in the Sun's output, can affect climate in general, the large majority of scientists conclude that the chief culprit in the current rapid warming is an increase in greenhouse gases in the atmosphere. The largest contributor is carbon dioxide, the concentration of which increased by about 25 percent during the 20th century, mainly owing to the burning of fossil fuels (mainly coal, petroleum, and natural gas).

In 2007 the Intergovernmental Panel on Climate Change forecast an increase in global mean temperature of between 3.2° and 7.2 °F (1.8° and 4.0 °C) by 2100 as compared to 1990, depending on various scenarios of future human activity. Leading climate scientists warn that the rising temperatures could have severe environmental and socioeconomic consequences. These warnings have

Rajendra Pachauri, the chair of the Intergovernmental Panel on Climate Change, in 2007. **AFP/Getty Images**

led to international efforts to minimize the threat, including policies designed to reduce the amount of greenhouse gases released into the atmosphere.

aggregate Taking all units as a whole.

altitude The vertical elevation of an object above a surface (as sea level or land) of a planet.

boreal Of, relating to, or located in northern regions.

coniferous Having, needle-shaped, or scale-like leaves and bearing cones; primarily describes evergreen trees or vegetation.

deciduous Shedding leaves during one season , typically the fall; usually describes broad-leaved trees.

equinox Either of the two moments in the year (about March 21 and September 23) when the Sun is exactly above the Equator and day and night are of equal length.

frigid Intensely cold.

insolation Exposure to the Sun's rays.

leaching The removal of elements from the top layer of soil by percolating water. The materials lost are carried downward and are generally redeposited in a lower layer.

leeward Being in or facing the direction toward which the wind is blowing.

mangrove Any tropical tree or shrub of the genus Rhizophora growing in marshes or tidal shores, noted for its interlacing above-ground roots.

mean Arithmetic average obtained by adding together all the scores or values and dividing the resulting sum by the number of cases.

monsoon A large-scale wind system that seasonally reverses its direction and is frequently accompanied by heavy rainfall.

percolate To ooze or trickle through a permeable substance; seep.

permafrost Perennially frozen ground with a temperature colder than 32 °F (0 °C) continuously for two or more years.

poleward Toward or in the direction of one of Earth's poles.

precipitation All liquid and solid water particles that fall from clouds and reach the ground, including drizzle, rain, snow, snow pellets, ice crystals, and hail.

relief The elevations or inequalities of a land surface.

saturation The presence in air of the most water possible under existent pressure and temperature conditions.

snow cover The amount of snow on the ground in a particular region.

snow line The lower boundary of permanent snow cover, the elevation of which depends on factors like wind, sun, temperature, and the amount of snowfall in a particular area.

solstice Either of the two moments in the year when the Sun's apparent path is farthest north or south from Earth's Equator, reached each year on about June 21 and December 21.

taiga Beginning at the southern edge of the tundra, a subarctic ecosystem characterized by conifers and a lichen-covered forest floor.

temperate Having a moderate climate that lacks extremes in temperature.

topography The configuration of a surface including its relief and the position of its natural and man-made features.

torrid Parched with heat especially of the Sun; hot.

trade wind Persistent wind that blows westward and toward the Equator from the subtropical high-pressure belts toward the intertropical convergence zone. The trade winds were named by the crews of sailing ships that depended on the winds during westward ocean crossings.

tundra An Arctic ecosystem defined by great expanses of treeless ground and a harsh, frigid climate.

undulating Moving in waves; fluctuating.

windward Being in or facing the direction from which the wind is blowing.

Climate Change
Environment Canada
Inquiry Centre
351 St. Joseph Boulevard
Place Vincent Massey, 8th Floor
Gatineau, QC K1A 0H3
Canada
(819) 997-2800
Web site: http://www.climatechange.gc.ca
Environment Canada provides information on the basics of climate and climate change as well as reports detailing the various issues Canadians face as a result of climate change and potential solutions.

Climate Institute
900 17th Street NW
Suite 700
Washington, DC 20006
(202) 552-4723
Web site: http://www.climate.org
The Climate Institute provides several games for those interested in understanding climate change as well as problem-solving ideas for those wishing to become more actively involved in issues related to climate and the environment.

Environmental Protection Agency
Ariel Rios Building
1200 Pennsylvania Avenue NW
Washington, DC 20460
(202) 272-0167
Web site: http://www.epa.gov
The Environmental Protection Agency
   offers interactive quizzes and games on
   its Web site to promote awareness of
   various ecological topics as well as project
   ideas for students who would like to take
   action on environmental issues in their
   own communities.

Joint Institute for the Study of the
   Atmosphere and Ocean
University of Washington
3737 Brooklyn Ave NE
Box 355672
Seattle, WA 98105
(206) 685-2899
Web site: http://www.jisao.washington.edu
The Joint Institute for the Study of the
   Atmosphere and Ocean offers informa-
   tion on various summer activities and
   programs for students interested in
   issues related to the atmosphere
   and climate.

National Oceanic and Atmospheric
   Administration
1401 Constitution Avenue NW
Room 5128
Washington, DC 20230
(301) 713-1208
Web site: http://www.noaa.gov
The National Oceanic and Atmospheric
   Administration provides information
   about opportunities to advance environ-
   mental literacy, including scholarships
   and internships for students.

National Snow and Ice Data Center
CIRES, 449 UCB
University of Colorado
Boulder, CO 80309
(303) 492-6199
Web site: http://nsidc.org
The National Snow and Ice Data Center offers
   information on the various aspects of
   snow and ice and how scientists set about
   researching the polar climates of the planet.

Natural Resources Canada
580 Booth
Ottawa, ON K1A 0E4
Canada

(613) 995-0947
Web site: http://www.nrcan-rncan.gc.ca/com
Natural Resources Canada offers access to
    its extensive library collection, and post-
    ers detailing the effects of climate change
    on Canada's various regions and indus-
    tries are available for download.

Pew Center on Global Climate Change
2101 Wilson Boulevard, Suite 550
Arlington, VA 22201
(703) 516-4146
Web site: http://www.pewclimate.org
The Pew Center on Global Climate Change
    provides helpful FAQs for students curi-
    ous about the basics of climate change
    and global warming as well as informa-
    tion on steps that can be taken to reduce
    their carbon footprint.

WEB SITES

Due to the changing nature of Internet links,
Rosen Educational Services has developed an
online list of Web sites related to the subject
of this book. This site is updated regularly.
Please use this link to access the list:

http://www.rosenlinks.com/ies/clim

Allaby, Michael. *Encyclopedia of Weather and Climate,* rev. ed. (Facts on File, 2007).

Burroughs, William, ed. *Climate: Into the 21st Century* (Cambridge Univ. Press, 2003).

Burroughs, W. J. *The Climate Revealed* (Cambridge Univ. Press, 1999).

Casper, J. K. *Water and Atmosphere: The Lifeblood of Natural Systems* (Chelsea House, 2007).

Cullen, Katherine. *Weather and Climate: The People Behind the Science* (Chelsea House, 2006).

Desonie, Dana. *Climate: Causes and Effects of Climate Change* (Chelsea House, 2007).

The Diagram Group. *Weather and Climate: An Illustrated Guide to Science* (Chelsea House, 2006).

Human, Katy, ed. *Critical Perspectives on World Climate* (Rosen, 2007).

Ochoa, George, and others. *Climate: The Force that Shapes Our World and the Future of Life on Earth* (Rodale, 2005).

Silverstein, Alvin, and others. *Weather and Climate* (Twenty-First Century Books, 2008).

Unwin, Mike. *Climate Change* (Heinemann Library, 2007).